STAR WARS™

A NEW HOPE

A long time ago, in a galaxy far, far away...a beautiful princess named Leia was fleeing from Darth Vader, a servant of the evil Empire. Leia and her Rebel friends had stolen the plans to the Empire's most terrible weapon, a gigantic space station called the Death Star. Just before she was captured by Vader, Leia gave the plans to the droid, R2-D2 who along with his friend C-3PO, managed to escape to the planet below.

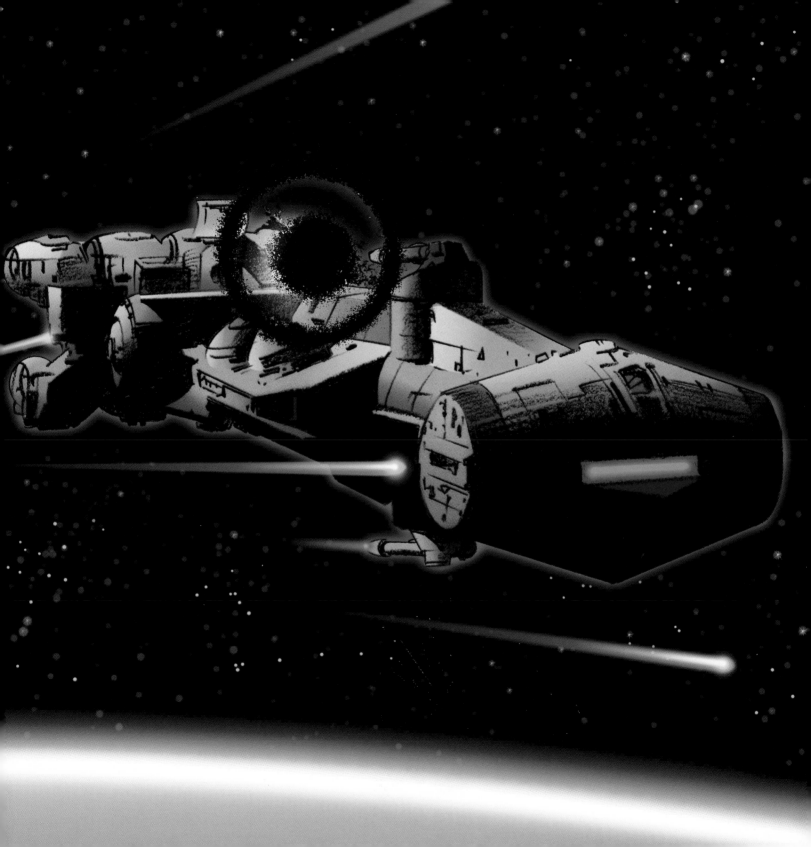

On the planet, the droids were quickly captured by Jawas, unpleasant little scavengers who sold them to Luke Skywalker. Luke was a brave young man who longed for adventure.

While cleaning R2-D2, Luke stumbled across the first part of a message from Princess Leia.

"It sounds like she's in trouble," Luke said. But R2-D2 would only play the rest of the message for someone named Obi-Wan Kenobi.

That night the plucky little droid set off across the dune sea to deliver the message himself.

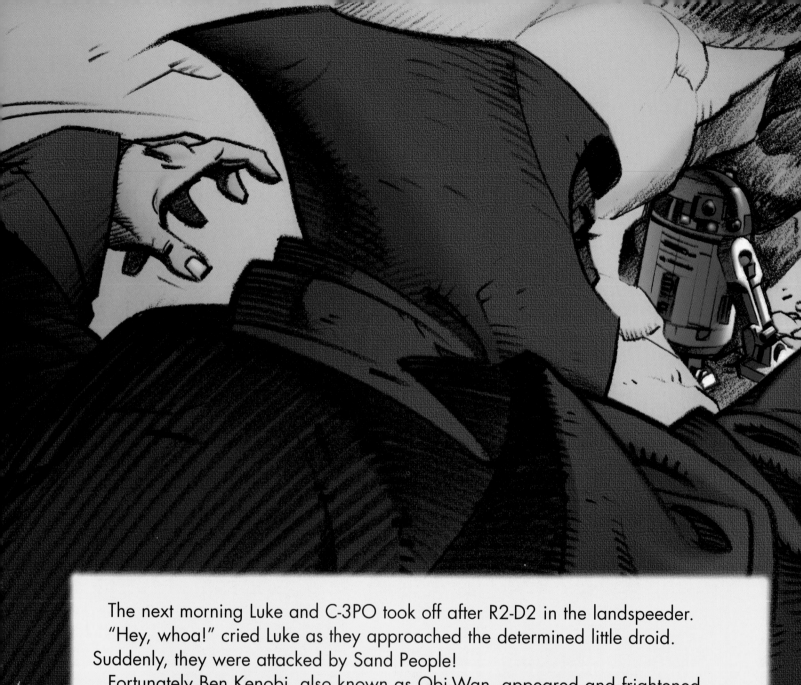

The next morning Luke and C-3PO took off after R2-D2 in the landspeeder. "Hey, whoa!" cried Luke as they approached the determined little droid. Suddenly, they were attacked by Sand People!

Fortunately Ben Kenobi, also known as Obi-Wan, appeared and frightened the Sand People away. "Rest easy—you've had a busy day," said Ben as he helped Luke up.

Back at Ben's dwelling, R2-D2 played Leia's desperate message. "Help me, Obi-Wan Kenobi, you're my only hope," Leia pleaded.

Ben explained to Luke that he and Luke's father had once been Jedi Knights, warriors who had guarded the galaxy for centuries. Their strength came from the Force, an energy field that unites all living beings in the galaxy. He gave Luke his father's lightsaber and encouraged him to join the fight against the Empire.

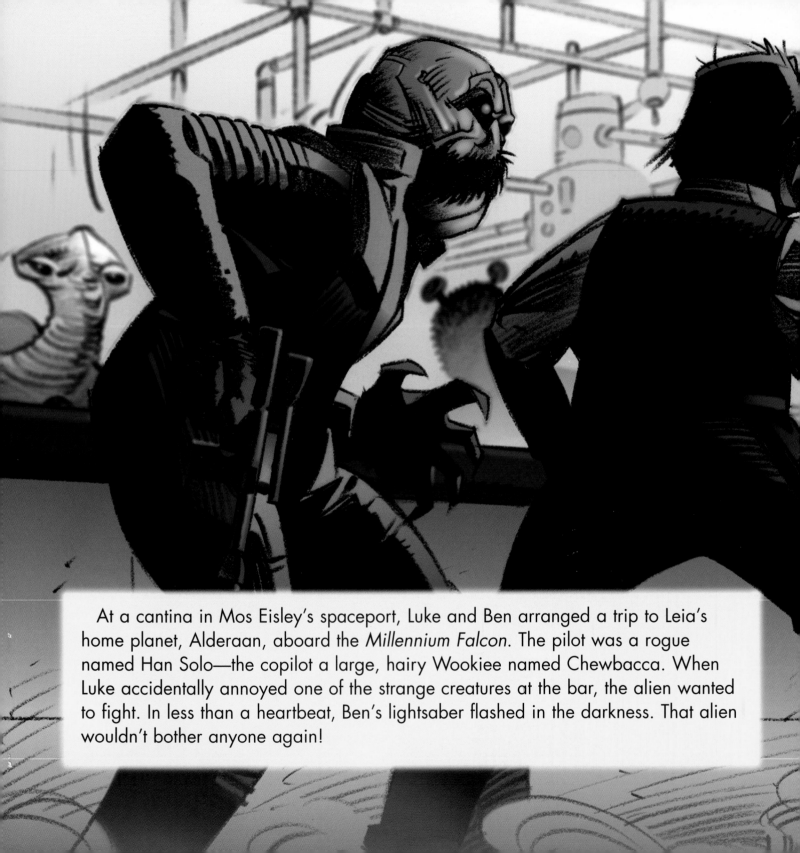

At a cantina in Mos Eisley's spaceport, Luke and Ben arranged a trip to Leia's home planet, Alderaan, aboard the *Millennium Falcon*. The pilot was a rogue named Han Solo—the copilot a large, hairy Wookiee named Chewbacca. When Luke accidentally annoyed one of the strange creatures at the bar, the alien wanted to fight. In less than a heartbeat, Ben's lightsaber flashed in the darkness. That alien wouldn't bother anyone again!

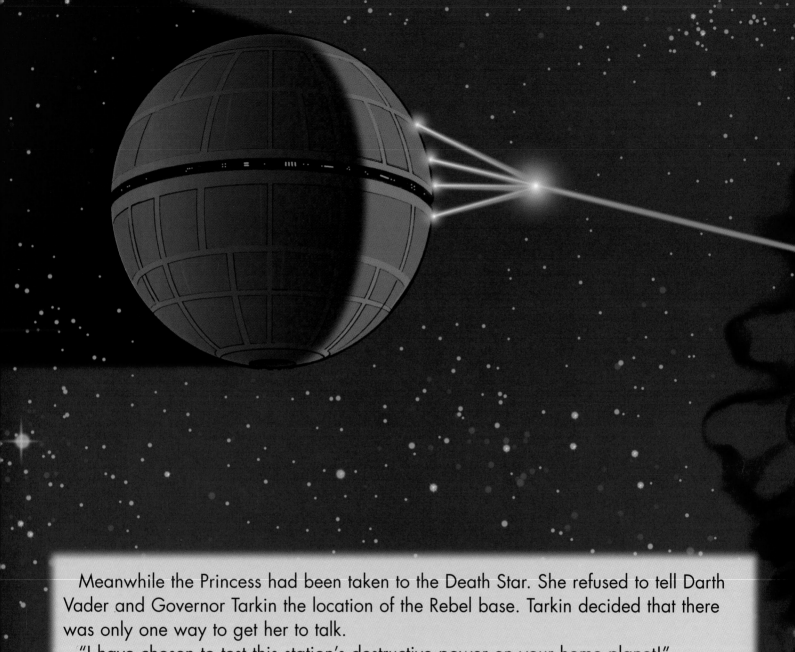

   Meanwhile the Princess had been taken to the Death Star. She refused to tell Darth Vader and Governor Tarkin the location of the Rebel base. Tarkin decided that there was only one way to get her to talk.

   "I have chosen to test this station's destructive power on your home planet!" he growled.

   "No, please, Alderaan is peaceful! You can't!" she begged, but it was too late. Alderaan was destroyed in a spectacular explosion!

When the *Millennium Falcon* popped out of hyperspace, Luke and his friends discovered that Alderaan was gone. Before they could change course, they were captured by a tractor beam and dragged onto the Death Star.

Luke, Han, and Chewie managed to outwit the Imperial stormtroopers and rescue Leia after a fierce blaster battle.

Meanwhile, Ben had freed the *Millennium Falcon* from the tractor beam and was on his way to rejoin his friends when he was stopped by Darth Vader!

"I've been waiting for you, Obi-Wan. Now I am the master," Vader said, the scarlet glow of his light saber reflecting off his jet black armor.

"Only a master of evil, Darth," Ben replied, lighting his saber.

The old foes attacked each other with grim determination. Ben finally sacrificed himself to ensure the safe getaway of his friends.

Quickly, Luke and his friends made their way to the secret Rebel base. There Luke and Leia prepared for the final battle, knowing that if they failed, darkness would descend over the entire galaxy.

Every Rebel pilot, except for Han and Chewie, took part in the attack on the Death Star. It was now only seconds from firing on the Rebel base.

As Luke lined up his shot, he heard Ben's voice urging him to use the Force. At that moment, Darth Vader moved his fighter into position directly behind Luke. "I have you now!" he roared.

At the last possible second, Han returned in the *Millennium Falcon* and his laser blast blew Darth Vader off course. Luke fired at the Death Star blowing it to pieces. "Great shot, kid!" yelled Han.

Back at the Rebel base a great ceremony was held. The newly polished C-3PO and R2-D2 gleamed as brightly as the medals Leia awarded to Luke and Han. Luke and his friends had saved the Rebel Alliance and won a major battle in the fight to free the galaxy from the evil Empire.

Little did they know that their adventures were just beginning, and they all looked to the future with a new hope!